365 DAYS OF HAPPINESS

Lizzie Cornwall

summersdale

365 DAYS OF HAPPINESS

Summersdale Publishers Ltd
46 West Street
Chichester
West Sussex
PO19 1RP
UK

www.summersdale.com

Printed and bound in the Czech Republic

ISBN: 978-1-84953-204-4

Substantial discounts on bulk quantities of Summersdale books are available to corporations, professional associations and other organisations. For details contact Summersdale Publishers by telephone: +44 (0) 1243 771107, fax: +44 (0) 1243 786300 or email: nicky@summersdale.com.

To Sarah B.

From Madison K.

So excited
for this Chapter
in our lives!

JANUARY

New Year's Day: host a Christmas present swap sale where friends and family can bring all their unwanted gifts and exchange them with each other – one man's trash is another man's treasure!

 Invent a make-believe life and tell your new hairdresser all about it – be as convincing as possible:

'I was a ballerina at the Bolshoi until I discovered heavy metal.'

JANUARY

'I can trace my ancestors back to the pharaohs of Egypt. See this birthmark? [show a birthmark or pen mark] King Tutankhamun had exactly the same one.'

 Enter every free competition you find. Increase your chances of winning that trip to New York by 100 per cent!

 Wolf-whistle a builder as you drive past them.

 Kiss someone in the rain. Don't settle for a soggy peck; go for a shoulder-grasping, music-inducing, slow-motion kiss.

JANUARY

 Overdress for the occasion.

 Google yourself and make a Wikipedia page so everyone can read about how great you are!

Elvis Presley's birthday: spend your day in a sparkly jumpsuit gyrating those hips!

 When it rains, put your wellies on, run outside and jump in the biggest puddle you can find.

10 Wear your pyjamas all day – yay!

 11 Learn to say 'I love you' in five languages:

Greek: *S'ayapo!*

Portuguese: *Eu te amo!*

Icelandic: *Ég elska þig!*

Russian: *Ja tebjá ljubljú!*

Swahili: *Nakupenda!*

And make sure you say each to your loved ones.

 12 Carry out a taste test: buy every brand of chocolate digestive and decide which one really tastes the best.

It's never too late to have a happy childhood.

Wayne Dyer

Change your thoughts and you change your world.

Norman Vincent Peale

15 Go to work dressed as your favourite cartoon superhero.

 16 Don't use the lift at work, don't take the stairs: slide down the bannister.

 17 Make a plaster cast of your foot. Give it to someone for their birthday, saying something like, 'I finally thought of the right thing to get you. You've always been so hard to buy for.'

Go to your local supermarket wearing only a full-length coat. Make sure it's fastened, of course – you don't want to get arrested!

 Use your best crockery, always. Every day is special.

 Research and learn some genuinely funny jokes.

'What's red with two legs?'

'Half a cat.'

21 Start a conga line while waiting for the bus.

 22 Eat the best ice cream you can get your hands on. In bed. Or in the bath.

 23 Sing at the top of your voice. It doesn't matter if you're off-key – unless you're auditioning for *The X Factor*, of course!

Write a love letter to your object of desire and post it. (Signing it is optional.)

Burns Night: celebrate the birth of the greatest Scottish poet by trying some haggis with neeps for dinner.

Australia Day: make sure you have a 'g'day' and enjoy everything Australian: playing the didgeridoo, listening to Kylie and having a barbie!

Optimism is the faith that leads to achievement. Nothing can be done without hope and confidence.

Helen Keller

28

Our life is what our thoughts make it.

Marcus Aurelius

29 Answer questions with questions.

 30 Make cupcakes and ice your initials on the tops. Savour them while watching aerobics on television.

 31 Watch a film that you used to love as a child.

FEBRUARY

 Say 'yes' to everything for a day.

 Correct all spelling and grammatical mistakes on everything you see with a red pen: menus, fliers, chalkboards, you name it.

 Go rambling.

Search Facebook for all the friends that you have lost touch with over the years and send them lovely messages.

 Be a tourist in your own town. Ride on an open-topped bus and photograph yourself flicking the V-sign in front of all the sights.

 Learn the dance moves from your favourite part of *Dirty Dancing* – stun your friends on the dance floor as you rock out to '(I've Had) The Time of My Life'!

Think like Sherlock Holmes and dissect every speck of information as you question where your partner has been when they arrive home five minutes late from work.

'I notice that your collar is one inch higher on the left than on the right and the knot in your tie is two-thirds smaller than when you left for work this morning…'

 Cycle from Land's End to John o'Groats (or just to St Ives) and eat fresh fish at the cafe on the beach.

 Sing all your conversations for the day.

Dream lofty dreams, and as you dream, so you shall become.

James Allen

One joy scatters a hundred griefs.

Chinese proverb

12

Darwin Day: claim to your friends and family that you've evolved an extraordinary power, like sensing cake from miles away or the ability to expel a foul-smelling gas to ward off predators.

 13 Write a letter to yourself, then hide it. Maybe in the pocket of a jacket you rarely wear?

14

Have a party on Valentine's Day for all your single friends. Send out handmade invites and spend the evening playing Cupid.

15 Smile, even when you don't feel like it.

 16 Sing into your friend's answering machine.

 17 Give things away that you don't want any more. Only the nicest things, though. Wrap them up beautifully and give them to friends, neighbours and family.

Grind your own coffee beans and try adding a few extra ingredients – a dash of chocolate powder, a pinch of cinnamon – and give your new creation an exotic name.

 Teach yourself how to do smoke rings – herbal cigarettes only, please.

 Learn the art of hypnotism. Start small by trying to put your pet in a trance, then build up to hypnotising your partner into making tea every time you say the word 'wibble'.

Pancake Day: get all your friends together for a massive Pancake Olympics in your garden.

Put Wham!'s greatest hits on the turntable, crank up the volume and jitterbug your way through the big spring clean.

Create a time capsule with photos, little notes and secrets and bury it in the garden with strict instructions that it mustn't be opened for at least ten years.

Always be ready to speak your mind, and a base man will avoid you.

William Blake

Every time you smile at someone it is an action of love, a gift to that person, a beautiful thing.

Mother Teresa

FEBRUARY

 26 Watch a complete season of *24* in one sitting.

 27 Walk to the highest point within a 5-mile radius of your house and see how many landmarks you can see. Perhaps do a sketch.

 28 Write that book. Plan it out, talk about it to a trusted friend and give yourself a deadline for finishing each chapter.

29

Leap Day: traditionally the day on which it is appropriate for women to propose. If you're not feeling so brave, make sure you tell that special person exactly how much they mean to you!

MARCH

1 Think of how many words rhyme with 'happy' and 'smile'.

2 Learn how to recognise some bird calls.

3 Make a three-course lunch to take to work, complete with crockery, cutlery and glasses. Treat yourself.

Get a bubble wand from a toyshop and see if you can make a bubble big enough for you to fit inside.

 Write multiple lists of everything you want – material possessions, relationships, work, lifestyle, everything. Pin them up by your door so you see them all the time. Better still, make a picture board to help you visualise them.

 Try a new type of tea.

He who enjoys doing and enjoys what he has done is happy.

Johann Wolfgang von Goethe

Happiness arises in a state of peace, not of tumult.

Ann Radcliffe

Throw yourself into a new creative project, something that you're excited about but which feels a little daunting. You'll be so consumed by it that it will fuel you for ages.

 Learn a traditional craft: sheep shearing, blacksmithing…

 Book a plane ticket to see that friend who moved away and who you always meant to visit.

Get your skates on and do circuits round the local park – much more fun than running!

 Feed the ducks at the local duck pond.

 Have a chocolate-themed dinner party: beef with savoury chocolate sauce, salad with cocoa nibs…

Build your dream house... out of Lego.

 Close your eyes, and randomly point to a dish on the menu rather than reading and choosing when you next go out to a restaurant.

St Patrick's Day: dress up as a leprechaun and finish every sentence with, 'To be sure!'

Mother's Day: give your mum a handmade card telling her how much she means to you. The more glue and glitter you use the better.

 Make an iPod playlist of all the cheesiest songs that you loved when you were 15.

 Seek out a book that you either really enjoyed or that inspired you and re-read it.

Turn your face to the sun and the shadows fall behind you.

Maori proverb

Humour is the great thing, the saving thing.

Mark Twain

Walk around smiling at everyone you pass – you'll be amazed at how many people will smile back.

 Re-watch your favourite childhood TV show.

Lady Day: until 1752, this day was the official start of the new year. If your year hasn't got off to the best start, consider this day as an opportunity to start over and face the rest of the year with a new enthusiasm!

Learn to read hieroglyphs, or at least pretend to know how to read them when you're next visiting the British Museum.

 Order a takeaway according to menu number only. Randomly pick five numbers and at least try each thing that you order.

 Hold a Twitter day where you have to respond to all messages in 140 characters or less.

29 Adopt a famous person's character and make all your decisions for the day based on this persona. Think: what would Churchill, Beckham, or Gandhi do?

 30 Ring your gran or catch up with another member of your family who you don't speak to very often.

 31 Count your blessings: literally. Make a list of everything in your life that you're thankful for.

APRIL

April Fool's Day: treat everything you hear as if it were an April Fool's trick.

'My tea's ready? Nah, you're having me on!'

 Next time the train is a bit too busy for your liking start having a conversation with yourself. Begin by whispering and get louder and louder until you have the desired amount of space around you.

The future belongs to those who believe in the beauty of their dreams.

Eleanor Roosevelt

Start by doing what's necessary; then do what's possible; and suddenly you are doing the impossible.

St Francis of Assisi

APRIL

 Spend your lunch hour in a lift, going up and down, saying hello and goodbye to everyone who gets in and out.

 Don your wellies and pac-a-mac and go on a bear hunt. Remember: you can't go over it, you can't go under it, so you'll have to go through it.

 Go through all of your old photo albums and find as many embarrassing and incriminating photos of friends and family as possible, and treat them to a slideshow.

Easter Sunday: devise the best ever Easter-egg hunt. Go all out with written clues, dead ends, and the biggest chocolate egg at the end of it.

 Sign up to do a challenge – whether it's the Marathon des Sables or a local fun run round the park.

 Grow or catch something to eat – whether it's a wild salmon or some cress for your egg sandwich.

Listen to your iPod from start to finish – no skipping those show tunes!

 Settle a disagreement at work with a dance-off.

 Anniversary of the first man in space: celebrate this historic day in mankind's history by getting a telescope and doing some stargazing.

Lie on your back in the garden, park or beach and watch the clouds change and make shapes.

 Go beachcombing and draw your finds.

 Go to the cinema and dress in something relating to the film you are seeing; for example: wear a wetsuit and flippers for an aquatic adventure, period costume for the latest bodice-ripper or paint yourself blue for *The Smurfs* or *Avatar.*

Illusory joy is often worth more than genuine sorrow.

René Descartes

18

Mix a little foolishness with your serious plans. It is lovely to be silly at the right moment.

Horace

Write funny messages in the dirt on cars. Or philosophical quotes, for example:

'We are all in the gutter, but some of us are looking at the stars.' Oscar Wilde

 Start a book club with your friends or, if you're not a big reader, start up a craft or comedy club; or just a gossip club. Or a pudding club!

The Queen's (actual) birthday: whenever you see/handle money, you must look adoringly at the Queen's portrait and declare your allegiance. Alternatively, spend the whole day singing 'God Save the Queen' by the Sex Pistols, gurning and spitting.

Dress like a supermodel for the school run – get a professional blow dry, put on fake tan (don't forget your hands), bling jewellery, shades, the highest heels you can walk in and a bodycon dress. Remember to give it some attitude as you strut to the school gate.

St George's Day: purchase a toy sword and spend the whole day slaying imaginary dragons.

APRIL

 Play fake-designer-handbag 'I spy' on Oxford Street.

 Prepare a poem, song, comedy routine or anything you like and perform it at an open-mic night.

 Give a beautiful bunch of Spring flowers to a friend and see their face light up!

Spend the whole day communicating in riddles.

'My first is in dungeon but not in deluge…'

 Spring clean the desktop on your computer and get rid of all those superfluous files and old emails. Find a special photo for your screensaver.

Never underestimate the power of passion.

Eve Sawyer

Satisfaction lies in the effort, not in the attainment. Full effort is full victory.

Mahatma Gandhi

MAY

May Day: two words: Morris dancing! Celebrate the heart and soul of English culture by covering yourself in bells, skipping around and hitting sticks together.

 Teach a niece/nephew/child of a friend a ridiculous untruth.

'Cheese is a type of vegetable; dogs will start to tap dance if you give them top hats and canes...'

Whilst on a bus, start singing 'The Wheels on the Bus' and encourage all the other passengers to join in.

 Organise a murder-mystery evening for you and your friends. Everyone has to come up with their own character, including an accent, a costume and an alibi.

 Hide in a box and deliver yourself to a friend's doorstep. Remember the air-holes!

 Make a finger- and sock-puppet menagerie and use them to act out an epic play from your own imagination.

7 Donate blood whilst dressed as a vampire.

8 Visit London and convince tourists that you are the real Big Ben.

9 Spend at least half the day making the best club sandwich ever.

10 Form a country in your living room. Create money, passports, a national anthem, a flag and everything a sovereign state needs. Be sure to keep your borders well guarded.

Come up with your own slang term and do your best to proliferate it as far as possible.

 Weed your neighbour's garden one night – without being spotted – so that it's immaculate by morning. Then, make a point of saying to them how lovely their garden looks. If you're feeling particularly generous, plant some beautiful flowers.

 Surprise a loved one by cooking a special supper, even if it is Alphabetti Spaghetti on toast (as long as it spells out their name!).

All great achievements require time.

Maya Angelou

15

The only journey is the one within.

Rainer Maria Rilke

16 Spend a day eating only foods of one colour, for example white: white bread, cooked egg-white, vanilla ice cream, white fish.

17 To break the monotony of the weekly shop why not undertake a supermarket sweep, set yourself a time limit and stick to it. List optional.

18

International Museum Day: take some time to visit a local museum today.

19 Learn to surf at your nearest beach – you'll be 'hanging ten' in no time!

 20 To brighten up a dull day in the office why not host an inaugural Office Olympics? Strive for the gold medal in the email relay or biro javelin.

 21 When you want to finish talking to an annoying colleague clamp your hands over your ears and say, 'La la la, I can't hear you' until they leave.

Challenge a colleague to move to another part of the office in the style of an animal of your choosing. For example: go to the photocopier as a kangaroo or the coffee machine as a crab, or the water cooler as an elephant.

 Take photos of all your favourite people and make an album.

 Compose a song about your favourite food and upload it to MySpace.

Plan a holiday to a destination in your home country.

 Write an anonymous blog about your workplace and circulate the link saying, 'Is someone here writing about me?'

 Hug a tree.

Sail away from the safe harbour. Catch the trade winds in your sails. Explore. Dream. Discover.

Mark Twain

You can break that big
plan into small steps and
take the first step
right away.

Indira Gandhi

Go to the children's playground and hog the swing for an hour.

 Laze in a hammock for the afternoon listening to your favourite chill-out music or a murder-mystery on the radio.

JUNE

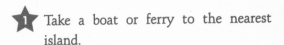 Take a boat or ferry to the nearest island.

2 Experiment with unusual flavours when making a batch of cakes: Pimm's and strawberries; chilli and chocolate.

3 Greet everyone with two kisses, one on each cheek.

4 Have a go at parkour (free-running) but build up gradually to running up walls.

First say to yourself what you would be; and then do what you have to do.

Epictetus

Find ecstasy in life; the mere sense of living is joy enough.

Emily Dickinson

JUNE

 Buy a Jew's harp and annoy everyone as you learn how to play it.

 Buy an old typewriter from a car boot sale and write anonymous love letters to a couple of single neighbours or work colleagues.

 Buy a cheap waterproof camera and a snorkel, head down to the beach and snap away underwater.

 Take pictures of unusually shaped clouds and find out whether they're cumulus, cirrus, altostratus…

JUNE

 Have a night-time picnic on a full moon in the garden or in the countryside and enjoy watching nocturnal comings and goings of wildlife, as well as admiring the stars while drinking wine and eating Scotch eggs!

 Get lost in your favourite city.

 Do something you were never allowed to do when you were young, like make a mud pie or eat a whole tub of ice cream, or wear a 'too-short' skirt and 'not-very-sensible' shoes.

 Walk the dog, or offer to walk a neighbour's dog if you don't have one.

Reach out to the people who inspire you but who don't know you exist.

Bloomsday: the day on which James Joyce's modernist epic *Ulysses* occurs. Celebrate by undertaking your own odyssey through a sprawling metropolis. Then, describe it in as much detail as you can, either with words or pictures.

Father's Day (third Sunday in June): whatever your dad's favourite hobby is – be it fishing, football or pottering around his shed – do it with him today.

Pick a warm, dry evening and pitch a tent in the garden. Think 'glamping' rather than Glastonbury: put a mattress in there along with some feather pillows, a duvet and some lamps with candles and enjoy the sounds of nature around you.

 As soon as you're up in the morning, write down five things that are brilliant about your life on a Post-it. Keep the Post-it in your bag or purse, somewhere where you'll see it throughout the day.

Midsummer's Eve: put on a donkey mask and ask everyone to call you 'Bottom'. You may yet find your true love, but don't get your hopes up when you look like an ass!

Attempt the impossible in order to improve your work.

Bette Davis

It is right to be contented
with what we have, but
never with what we are.

James Mackintosh

Speak as fast as you can to someone (don't worry if you stumble over your words) and then ask if they got all that. If they didn't, say, 'Your loss. I haven't got time to repeat it all.'

 Learn synchronised swimming – keep smiling even when you've swallowed half the pool.

 Stay up all night/get up early to watch the sunrise. And greet it like a cockerel would.

JUNE

 26 Find out the birthday of your favourite famous person and devote an entire day to them: dress up like them; if they're a musician, listen only to their music; if they are a writer quote them. Invite all of your friends to a party in honour of your chosen person.

 27 Camp out in the queue for Wimbledon, then spend your day cheering for the underdog and enjoying strawberries and cream.

 28 Have an evening summer picnic in the park with your friends. Go somewhere with a hill for rolling down!

Fall seven times, stand up eight.

Japanese proverb

30

Some run swiftly; some creep painfully; all who keep on will reach the goal.

Piyadassi Thera

JULY

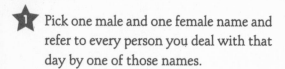

⭐**1** Pick one male and one female name and refer to every person you deal with that day by one of those names.

⭐**2** Write a really embarrassing appointment in a colleague's (or, even better, your boss's) diary.

⭐**3** Go to a public place such as a park, square or even a bus stop and start dancing. See if you can get other people to join your flash mob. This is particularly successful if you take a group of friends along.

JULY

American Independence Day: celebrate finally being rid of those pesky Thirteen Colonies and indulge in something American, be it a season of *Friends*, a game of baseball or a packet of twinkies.

Tynwald Day: the national day of the Isle of Man. Celebrate this magnificent island by spending the day singing songs by its favourite sons: the Bee Gees.

Spend the day lounging in a paddling pool in your garden.

 Commit to making every recipe in your favourite recipe book over the course of a year à la *Julie and Julia*.

 If you can't afford to go to Glastonbury have your own festival and name it after yourself: the Festival of Me has a certain ring to it! Organise games and music for family and friends.

Go on a wine-tasting weekend and bluff your way through by slurring such phrases as, 'I smell baby socks and two-day-old takeaway chicken korma,' before downing each glass in one.

 Vow not to email or text your partner for a week, but call them or leave them handwritten love notes to find; and we're not talking, 'What's for dinner?'

 Enjoy a day in a local wood and pick leaves to identify when you get home.

Regret for wasted time is more wasted time.

Mason Cooley

Aim for the moon. If you miss, you may hit a star.

W. Clement Stone

JULY

14

Bastille Day: a day to celebrate everything French. Enjoy cheese, wine, the accordion, and having a certain *je ne sais quoi.*

15

St Swithin's Day: according to tradition, the weather on St Swithin's Day will remain for 40 days. Spend all day outside to accustom yourself to the weather to come.

16 Find out exactly what's growing in your garden and draw out a map with labels pinpointing each plant.

Make a sand sculpture on the beach and take photos of your handiwork as the tide comes in.

 Get three envelopes and write three different denominations on three pieces of paper – such as £5, £50, £150 – and on three consecutive Saturdays pick an envelope and allow yourself to spend whatever amount is inside.

 Write achievable 'New Month resolutions' at the start of every month – far less daunting than a list of New Year's resolutions.

Give yourself the singular responsibility of completing the *Times* crossword for today.

 When you've done something that you're particularly proud of – produced a great piece of artwork, received a job offer or pay rise or have been praised for doing something really good – buy yourself something small like a badge or a picture that will remind you of your achievement for years to come.

Part your hair in a different way or try a topknot.

 Spend some time working out what those six degrees of separation are between you and your greatest living hero.

 Go boating, and don't forget to look out for Ratty and Toad.

He who sows courtesy reaps friendship, and he who plants kindness gathers love.

St Basil of Caesarea

26

Happiness is not something ready-made. It comes from your own actions.

Dalai Lama

Try out different superstitions on days when you need an extra bit of luck – such as a job interview or even when you buy a lottery ticket – to see which one works. You could try looking at the new moon over your shoulder, carrying a rabbit's foot or avoiding walking on the cracks in the pavement.

 Spend a whole day making the most impressive sandcastle you can. Take photos and then jump all over it.

29 Make a habit of pausing every hour to remember the occasions when you really belly-laughed – it's the good times that will make you smile.

 30 Eat watermelon in the sunshine and try to spit the pips into a pot – goodbye manners and decorum, hello fun.

 31 Organise a street party and get to know your neighbours.

AUGUST

Yorkshire Day: celebrate this northern county by ensuring everything you eat is served in a Yorkshire pudding.

Disconnect the phone, let your mobile battery die, muffle the doorbell and spend the day pretending you are on a desert island.

Find a pond or stream and lose yourself watching dragonflies, water boatmen, fish and frogs – it's nature's answer to meditation.

AUGUST

 Start a rumour at the airport – 'I just saw Tom Cruise heading towards Gate 28' – and watch it ripple through the crowd.

 Have a water fight on a hot summer day. Get inventive with water receptacles: watering cans, old squeezy bottles, balloons.

 Indulge in afternoon tea: jam and scones, clotted cream, hot-buttered crumpets, cake and tea from a pot (with a flouncy tea cosy).

Great things are not
done by impulse, but by a
series of small things
brought together.

George Eliot

True happiness comes from the joy of deeds well done, the zest of creating things new.

Antoine de Saint-Exupéry

9 Bake bread, brew coffee, build up a nice warm fug and enjoy the sense of well-being the smell brings.

 10 Learn origami. Fold all of your £10 notes into swans and pay with them.

 11 Try brass-rubbing in a church or cathedral – release your inner soul.

Play on the roundabout in the local park, then see if you can walk in a straight line.

International Lefthander's Day: if you're a lefty, revel in it. If not, try experiencing how the other 10 per cent live and use your left hand as much as possible.

 Try dowsing for water or ley lines.

Toast marshmallows after a barbecue
– if you are feeling really decadent,
tear up a chunk of condensed jelly for
skewering.

 Surprise a friend at work and take them
out to lunch.

 Sign up for the Mongol Rally.

18 Go for a Turkish bath.

 19 Find a really big horizon to look into. The less detail to invade your eye space the further you can sink into reverie.

 20 Rearrange all the furniture in your house – it'll feel like you've moved!

21

Happiness consists not in having much, but in being content with little.

Marguerite Gardiner

I think I began learning
long ago that those who
are happiest are those
who do the most
for others.

Booker T. Washington

23 Host a clothes-swap party – invite your friends to bring their wardrobe cast-offs and swap your old things for theirs – out with the old and in with the new!

 24 Run away with the circus, or learn to juggle.

 25 Learn to make sushi.

Take seven pairs of pants and embroider each with a day of the week.

 Go to a bed shop and have a 5-minute snooze on every display bed.

 Learn to make the perfect cappuccino. Make you and your partner one to take to work in a travel cup every morning for a week. Make biscotti, too, if you're feeling particularly generous.

29 Buy some fish and chips and cycle to your nearest beach or lake to enjoy them.

 30 Knit your pet a jumper – a snake would look particularly fetching in a stripy one-piece, for example!

 31 Forage elderflower heads and flash-fry them with butter – tastes even better when they're free!

SEPTEMBER

1 Attack that chair or sideboard that you've always hated with paint, wallpaper and some lovely fabric to give it a new lease of life.

2 Make bunting and string it up everywhere: your garden, your bathroom, your car…

3 Drench your lawn with water and go aqua-planing.

If you want to be happy, be.

Leo Tolstoy

Independence is happiness.

Susan B. Anthony

Photocopy a body part and give it pride of place on the fridge door.

 Shake off that back-to-school feeling by hitting the beach at the weekend.

 On a windy day, grab an umbrella and pretend to be Mary Poppins.

9 To really get to know what's going on in your friends' heads, play word association games.

 10 Put on a silly accent and call up your friends. See who takes the longest to work out it's you.

 11 Have a cardboard-tube swordfight!

Learn to do shadow puppets on a sunny day against a white wall.

International Chocolate Day: as if an excuse to indulge in chocolate was ever needed!

 Make a rag rug out of old clothes that you can't bring yourself to throw away – could be a child's first outfit, a special dress – then you will have them forever.

15 Tackle Shakespeare for the first time since your school days – you'll be amazed how funny it is!

 16 Go UFO-spotting.

 17 Adopt an animal at the local zoo or wildlife sanctuary.

18

There are two ways of spreading light: to be the candle or the mirror that reflects it.

Edith Wharton

Those who bring sunshine into the lives of others cannot keep it from themselves.

J. M. Barrie

20 Make the longest daisy chain ever.

 21 Buy a sketchbook and the next time you want to record something, draw it instead of photographing it.

 22 Try to go a whole day without saying anything negative.

 23 Wake up early enough on an autumn morning to watch the dew sparkling in sunlight on yesterday's cobwebs.

SEPTEMBER

 On a sunny day, make temporary pictures with water and a brush on your patio.

 Dig out your postcards from exotic destinations that you never got round to writing and post them out to friends and family.

 Try a new type of fruit.

 Hide yourself away in your shed, kitchen, or anywhere your mind can work at its best and create an invention that will change the world!

SEPTEMBER

 Revisit a childhood holiday destination.

 Send a message in a bottle out to sea. Make sure you add your address to the note – you never know, someone might write back!

 Create a rockery in your garden where amphibious creatures can hibernate in winter.

OCTOBER

1 Go in search of your soul mate. If you've already found them, do they know?

2 Try your hand at an extreme sport.

3 People-watch in your local high street. Make up back-stories for the people you like the look of.

He who knows that enough is enough will always have enough.

Lao Tzu

You will never be happier
than you expect. To
change your happiness,
change your expectation.

Bette Davis

Come up with an amusing pseudonym to use when booking tables at restaurants and signing guest books.

 Create a design and stencil it onto a T-shirt.

 Research your family tree.

Invite all your friends to a traditional children's party. Essentials include jelly and ice cream, Pin the Tail on the Donkey and Pass the Parcel.

 Try on wedding dresses, or top hats and morning suits.

 Go all out and cook the best roast dinner ever.

Have a go at brewing your own beer.

 Stock up on coins and visit the amusement arcade.

 Start a hand-written correspondence with a distant relative.

Find an unusual receptacle for planting flowers or herbs, such as an old pair of wellies, or a watering can.

 Find a beech tree in the autumn and rustle through the leaves like you did when you were five.

 Visit a petting zoo.

Collect as precious pearls
the words of the wise
and virtuous.

Abd-el-Kadar

All animals, except man, know that the principal business of life is to enjoy it.

Samuel Butler

20 Write limericks about people you know.

 21

Apple Day: a day to celebrate 'local distinctiveness'. Find the nearest orchard and do a bit of old-fashioned scrumping.

 22 Fish out those dog-eared old playing cards and remind yourself of how to play Clock Patience – much more satisfying than the computer version.

23 Try a new type of cheese.

 24 Make a rope swing or hammock.

 25

Anniversary of Chaucer's death: make your own pilgrimage to a place of personal significance, be it where you were born, where your family came from, a location from your favourite film or where your favourite band played their first gig.

Customise your clothes. Rhinestones and sequins will never go out of style.

 Eat honey straight from the jar.

 Make something out of papier mâché.

29 Spend the day wearing a onesie.

30 Invite friends over and play old-fashioned parlour games, such as charades and blind man's buff.

31

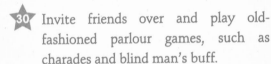

Halloween: go for a midnight walk through a graveyard and scare yourself silly!

NOVEMBER

 Go on a tandem bike ride with a friend.

 Spend some time finding the best hide-and-seek locations in your home.

 Read a book purely on the merit of someone's recommendation.

 Learn to knit or crochet.

Bonfire Night: fireworks are passé! Commemorate the plot to blow up Parliament by creating a scale model of the House of Lords to explode, or re-stage the events by acting out a play for your friends and family. And if you really want fireworks that much, they can be your finale.

Have a party where all the attendees have to carry out certain feats and challenges.

7

Your imagination is
your preview of life's
coming attractions.

Albert Einstein

What we plant in the soil of contemplation, we shall reap in the harvest of action.

Meister Eckhart

Draw a tattoo onto your arm/neck/face with a pen and visit your parents.

 Get all your old board games out and spend the day playing them. Who's for Mousetrap?

 Write a letter to your favourite teacher from school, letting them know how much they inspired you to become the person you are.

Orchestrate your own brief encounter at a railway station with your amour.

 Give your life a soundtrack by humming mood-appropriate music throughout the day.

 Take all the items you intend to use in a day and wrap them up like presents, so you can open them when you need them.

Obstacles are those frightful things you see when you take your eyes off your goal.

Henry Ford

16

Small opportunities are often the beginning of great enterprises.

Demosthenes

Plant daffodil bulbs in a heart shape in the autumn and wait for the love to appear next spring.

Mickey Mouse's birthday: inhale helium and do your best Mickey Mouse impersonation.

 Ride down a flight of stairs on a mattress.

 Have a massage. (You'll need it after riding down the stairs!)

Do some exercise to allow you to have an even bigger slice of cake.

 While a friend or loved one is asleep, paint their face as a cat/dog/Spider-Man.

 Pick some sloes and make sloe gin.

 Create a short stop-motion film.

25 Make your own guacamole.

 26 Speak like Yoda for a day. Very amusing it is!

 27 Dedicate a day to colouring-in.

 28 Challenge a friend to an arm-wrestling match. The loser has to buy lunch.

Resolve to take a photo every day for a year and create an album to look back on.

 Pick a letter of the alphabet and base your daily activities around it. Example: 'C' – go to the cinema, preferably to see a film beginning with 'c', then go to a cafe for a cup of coffee and a slice of carrot cake – do all of this whilst wearing a cloak. And if you want to stretch the rules, take a trip to the sea.

DECEMBER

 Have a tea party with some teddy bears.

 Act like you're being followed by an invisible TV crew for a day. Tell everyone that you come into contact with that there are hidden cameras everywhere and see how they react.

 Audition for the annual pantomime at your local amateur dramatics society.

DECEMBER

 Make up maxims using Beatles' lyrics and drop them into conversations:

'Well, we can't get to Strawberry Fields without first going through Penny Lane.'

'Rain at first light brings a hard day's night.'

 When chaos and pandemonium reign, firmly wedge in ear plugs and smile at your inner peace.

 Go to your city centre and give out free hugs/high fives.

 Dye your hair a crazy colour. Perhaps a festive red or green?

Think of all the beauty still left around you and be happy.

Anne Frank

Happiness often sneaks in
through a door you didn't
know you left open.

John Barrymore

DECEMBER

 Dress up in Victorian-style clothing and go carol singing.

 Excavate a small patch of your garden and record what you find.

 Take the afternoon off and indulge in your 'guilty pleasures', whatever they may be – cocktails, chocolate cake, old episodes of *Murder, She Wrote*, romcoms, etc.

 Spend an afternoon in your local library.

Illuminate your house with candlelight.

 Write a round robin letter to send to all of your annoying friends who write each year to say how wonderful their children are. Make yours as disappointing as possible:

'Tom has turned his back on the Church and is now an international arms dealer. Matt is in prison, and I lost a leg while riding a merry-go-round...'

 Bring back robotic dancing at the next party you attend.

17

A journey of a thousand miles begins with a single step.

Lao Tzu

There is no chance,
no destiny, no fate,
Can circumvent or
hinder or control
The firm resolve of a
determined soul.

Ella Wheeler Wilcox, from 'Will'

DECEMBER

19

Jane Austen's birthday: act as a matchmaker for your single friends, and pretend to swoon if anybody does anything even slightly uncouth.

20

Hire a snow machine and transform your garden into a winter wonderland.

21

Winter Solstice: the shortest day of the year. The day's so short you might as well make like a small mammal and hibernate, and build up your reserves for the onslaught of the festive season.

Get up early and take photos of frost on the grass and leaves in your garden.

 Make paper-chains from Sunday supplements.

 Dress up in your smartest outfit and enjoy dinner *à deux* with a loved one at the local fast-food restaurant.

DECEMBER

25

Christmas Day: enjoy the peace and quiet of a long walk or cycle in the countryside – best get it in before lunch, though!

26

Boxing Day: not just about leftovers! This used to be a day when service people and tradesmen were given gifts and thanks for their work throughout the year. Why not bring back this noble tradition?

27 Go ice-skating in a Lycra jumpsuit.

Hire a sports car for the day and take a drive past friends' houses, tooting loudly as you pass them.

 Make a crumble with seasonal fruits.

 Lie down in the snow, stretch out your arms above your head and bring them to your sides to make snow angels.

Go confidently in the direction of your dreams. Live the life you have imagined.

Henry David Thoreau